Mony Doyle and Glen Doyle
Illustrations by Ekaterina Alkushina

The Day The Zoo Went Quiet

Bumblebee Books
London

BUMBLEBEE PAPERBACK EDITION

Copyright © Mony Doyle and Glen Doyle 2021
Illustrations by Ekaterina Alkushina

The right of Mony Doyle and Glen Doyle to be identified as author of
this work has been asserted in accordance with sections 77 and 78 of the Copyright,
Designs and Patents Act 1988.

All Rights Reserved

No reproduction, copy or transmission of this publication
may be made without written permission.
No paragraph of this publication may be reproduced,
copied or transmitted save with the written permission of the publisher, or in accordance
with the provisions
of the Copyright Act 1956 (as amended).

Any person who commits any unauthorised act in relation to
this publication may be liable to criminal
prosecution and civil claims for damage.

A CIP catalogue record for this title is
available from the British Library.

ISBN: 978-1-83934-215-8

Bumblebee Books is an imprint of
Olympia Publishers.

First Published in 2021

Bumblebee Books
Tallis House
2 Tallis Street
London
EC4Y 0AB

Printed in Great Britain

www.olympiapublishers.com

Dedication

To Aidan and Anya. Our inspiration. Our Life.

For the animals at the zoo every day was a busy day. There were different faces every day. Sometimes even the same face more than once, even though only Elephant could remember.

"Imagine what it must feel like to eat my lunch in peace," said Panda. "People, people... and more people all day long!" Elephant heard that and added, "They even watch me have a bath! Is it too much to ask for a bit of privacy?"

Monkey didn't mind them much when they gave him bananas but since that silly 'No Feeding the Animals' sign had been put up the fun was over! "Faces, faces and more faces... and no bananas!" he complained.

"I am certainly tired of sharing my exuberance with that lot," said Lion rearranging his mane.

Every day was the same. Busy, busy, busy. Noise, noise, noise! Except for one particular sunny day. An ordinary day like any other. They woke up and had their breakfast as usual. They waited for the crowd as usual. But something changed. The crowd didn't come!

The zoo went completely quiet. At first they thought it was just luck but the days passed and nothing changed. "What's going on?" cawed Cockatoo flying over the zoo looking for the people for the tenth time that day.

"I don't know but it suits me fine," said Panda munching on her bamboo leaves without peering eyes on her.

"Finally I can wake up and not worry if I have a bad mane day," agreed Lion.

"Feels like being back in the jungle," said Elephant getting a body scrub in privacy.

Monkey chuckled and almost reminded Elephant that there was no body scrubbing in the jungle but thought better of it. Besides, he was distracted. He had started to miss the faces and the noise.

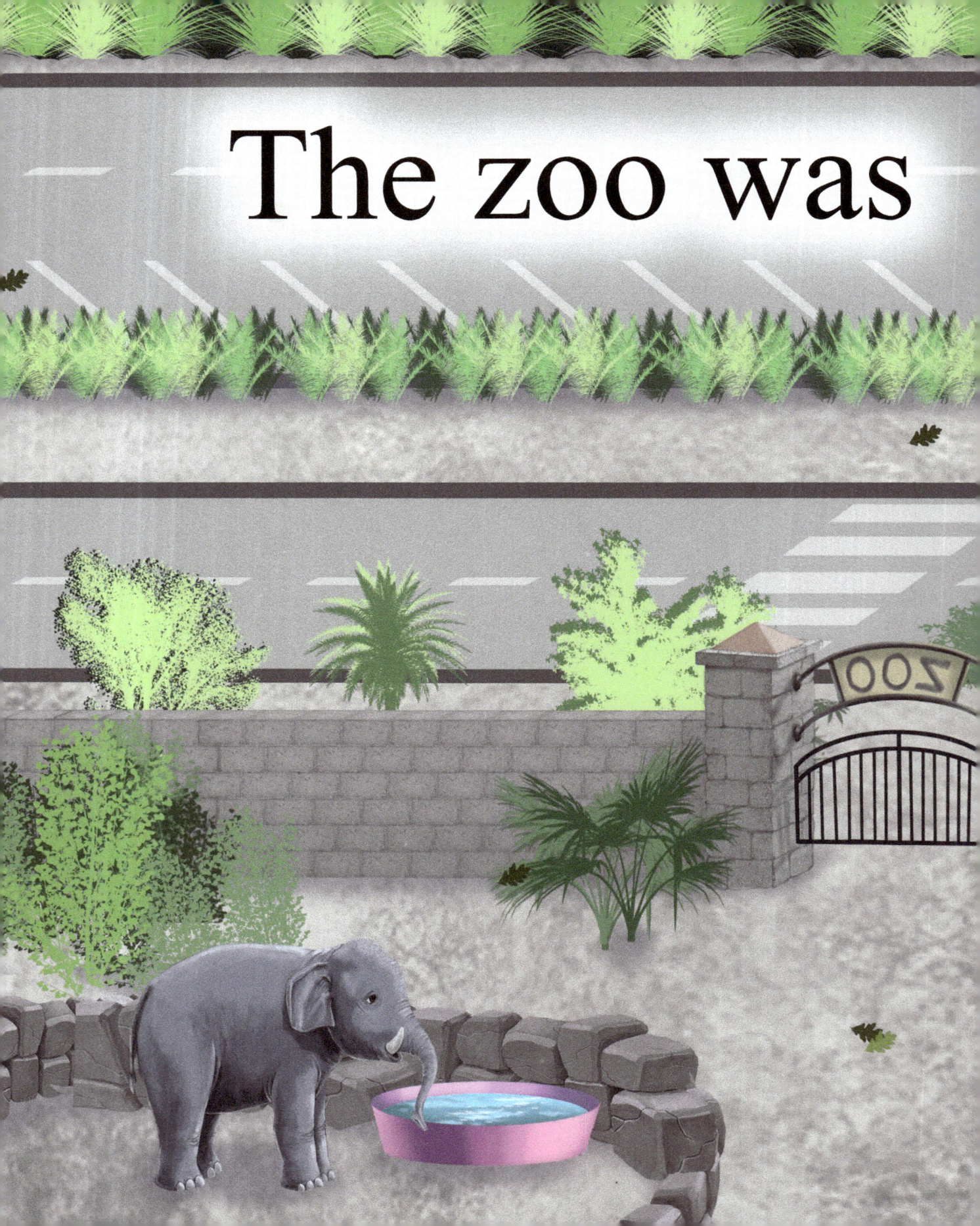
The zoo was

just too quiet.

After a while the animals started to wonder where the people went. A strange feeling took hold of them. They started to feel lonely.

The animals started to get daily updates from Cockatoo. "No, no sign of humans yet. But I've heard a new word many times. 'Corona'," he added.

"Corona?" they all repeated.
"Sounds like an animal," said shy Panda who never thought she would actually miss people. She had decided she had had enough privacy. She felt abandoned.

"It must be a splendid animal to keep all the humans away from the zoo for so long," said proud Lion who secretly enjoyed the people admiring his majestic mane. He felt jealous.

Playful Monkey who had no one to laugh at his monkey tricks felt neglected.

Elephant who could be a bit of a grump finally admitted to missing the smiles that the little humans used to give her every day. And as she could not forget, she felt sad.

One thing was for sure, none of them liked this 'Corona'. Not one bit! According to Cockatoo not even the zookeepers said good things about it and they usually liked all animals!

The zookeepers were also wearing strange face masks which convinced the animals 'Corona' must also smell bad. The animals at the zoo came to the conclusion that 'Corona' was a mean, smelly, selfish animal that stole all the fun from them. And the longer they went without people, the more they didn't like it.

"I think I wouldn't mind having the people back," admitted Panda. "I would even share some of my bamboo with them."

"I would put on a fabulous water show for them if they came back and even smile back at the little ones," said Elephant.

"I would give them my bananas. All of them," sulked Monkey.

"And I promise I would stop roaring at the little ones to give them a fright just for fun," regretted Lion.

Then one day something extraordinary happened. The day began like any other day as usual. They woke up and had their breakfast as usual. There was no excitement. There was no one to wait for. But then... An excited caw from Cockatoo broke the silence, "People are coming back! People are coming back!" And he was right! People were coming back!

Although they were behaving a little strangely. They kept a certain distance from one another. Not that humans behaving strangely surprised the animals at all! After all humans were a strange lot.

There was just one thing that they couldn't understand. Even though the animals themselves couldn't smell a thing, all the human faces were covered in masks.

"Is it us?" they thought. "Couldn't be, we've all had a bath!"

They looked at Warthog who was infamous for stinking the whole zoo sometimes. But he swore it wasn't him. Not this time! "This 'Corona' beast must smell really bad! Thank goodness it didn't come to live at the zoo," they thought, smiling at their much missed audience.

And there was another thing about the humans the animals hadn't noticed until now.

Even though the animals couldn't see their smiles through the masks, they learned that humans could smile with their eyes.

And that made all the animals

at the zoo very happy indeed.

About the Author

Mony and Glen are proud parents who, like all parents, had to find creative ways to explain a pandemic to their children.
They found a way through stories.
One day their daughter said, "I miss the Zoo."
"I bet the animals miss you too," they said.
And this is how *The Day The Zoo Went Quiet* came to be, from a bedtime story to a book.

Acknowledgements

To all the parents who like us had to step up and ride the wave. To all the children and their resilience and determination to thrive through adversity.

To Ekaterina Alkushina and her tireless efforts to create the perfect background to our tale.

www.ingramcontent.com/pod-product-compliance
Lightning Source LLC
LaVergne TN
LVHW072013060526
838200LV00059B/4669